Spiritual Enemies Behind Relationships and Marriages

Apostle John Laichena

Spiritual Enemies Behind Relationships and Marriages
Apostle John Laichena

John Laichena Publishing
Washington, D.C.

Library of Congress Control Number: 2016913463
Copyright © 2016 Apostle John Laichena
ISBN: 978-1-940243-99-3

All rights reserved. No part of this book may be reproduced without written permission from the publisher or copyright holder, except in the case of brief quotations embodied in critical articles and reviews. No part of this book may be transmitted in any form or by any means—electronic, mechanical, photocopy, recording or other—without prior written permission from the publisher or copyright holder.

Unless otherwise indicated, all Scripture quotations designated (NIV) are taken from the Holy Bible, New International Version® NIV® Copyright © 1973, 1978, 1984, 2011 by Biblica, Inc.® Used by permission. All rights reserved worldwide.

Contents

Chapter One................................. 1
Spiritual witchcraft breaking relationships and marriages
Witchcraft confusions and separations

Chapter Two 7
People the devil uses to destroy someone's life
Maidservants and relatives
Media and the bigger community crisis catching up with kids

Chapter Three 13
A child is a great nation
Spiritual war between traditions and Christianity
Circumcision rituals and satanism

Chapter Four 21
The bond between relationships and marriages
What is diverting and delaying spirits in a relationship?
Reasons devils use to delay or divert relationships

Chapter Five 27
Wedding happiness and an ugly demon of divorce
Gifts given during a wedding day becoming a spiritual attack later
Immoral past attacking your future happiness

Chapter Six 37
Married couples must be respected by all people
A traditional African Girl in an engagement
A relationship is a hidden treasure for you to discover

Chapter Seven 47
Taking a risk by faith to get the man or woman you love
My personal testimony about the faithfulness of God in a relationship

Chapter Eight. 53
Marriage and challenges involved
The enemies of a happy marriage
Revealed secrets behind relationships and marriages

Introduction

"The sovereign Lord is my strength; he makes my feet like the feet of a deer, he enables me to tread on the heights" (Habakkuk 3:19, NIV). This is a message of hope to someone in a troubled relationship or marriage. It is the devil who causes confusion in our families, possessing people with sadness. It is only God who can deliver people from satanic attacks in Jesus's name. Parents may notice weird behaviors in the lives of their kids as they grow.

There are spiritual enemies behind relationships and marriages

Punishing or taking your kids for counselling because of satanic attacks cannot help that much because their problems are spiritual. It is your responsibility as a parent to know what your kids are watching in the media or reading in magazines. If we do not teach our children the right way, someone else will show them the wrong way.

Introduction

Chapter One

Spiritual witchcraft breaking relationships and marriages Witchcraft confusion and separations

Some years back after Sunday service, Mercy approached me in tears. I remember it so clearly. She told me a very touching story about how she was left by her fiancée after being in a relationship with him for eight years. Her fiancée disappeared with another woman secretly and refused to receive her phone calls. Mercy started telling me the details of the nightmare she had before his disappearance. In the dream, people she knew visited her family with a cow and said it was Mercy's dowry for their son, who was a lunatic. The following day, she found the same cow standing in the same place it was in the dream. Before she explained anything to anybody, the cow moved away to the woods. Many people may not understand satanic attacks individuals undergo in their dreams because of spiritual blindness. Mercy was left with many questions in her heart about the cow in the dream and in the physical.

After some days, the madman who was in the dream visited her house in the physical world. He told her, "Mercy, you are my wife," and then he walked away. Mercy needed divine intervention from God because she was in great distress. After prayer, she received peace to wait for the perfect will of God in her life. She found another fiancée who married her later.

Nightmares are spiritual attacks from the dark world planned by spiritual beings using dark powers of witchcraft. It is hard to for us understand the spiritual things using our carnal mind. Prayer is the only way to defeat the enemy in Jesus's name. We cannot see these spirits with our physical eyes, but we can experience their torments in the spiritual world. A demon-possessed person cannot set himself or herself free from the bondage of the satanic kingdom. He or she needs a pastor to pray for her or him in Jesus's name. There is power in the blood of Jesus.

How do these demonic spirits possess the spirit and the body? The devil uses satanic ways such as witchcraft or generational curses to channel people into the dark world. Naming kids after people has deeper meaning in the spiritual. If you are named after a witch, murderer, thief, or prostitute, you will have the same spirits in both the spiritual and physical. We need to choose blessed names for our kids and take them to the church for ordination. Covenanting our children with the blood of Jesus builds a strong wall of protection in our life. We can't blame people for spiritual things they didn't know; it is only God who can give someone peace in Jesus's name.

At times, kids go through scary dreams which makes them wake up sweating and screaming. We should not make fun of nightmares in the lives of our kids. We need to pray for them in Jesus's name. For us to understand spiritual things, we have to be a spirit-filled Christian. It is only the blood of Jesus that can fight spiritual battles in our lives. We have to teach our kids the ways of God as they grow. Devil worshipping is real. Witches attend church fellowships secretly to cause confusion during sermons so that the brethren may not listen to the Word of God

Dorcas broke many relationships and stopped many weddings using her magic powers of witchcraft. Dorcas possessed many ladies with demonic spirits of barrenness by arresting their menses with her dark powers of witchcraft.

She revealed to me how she was without menses for years. She would experience spiritual animals that sacked her menstrual blood for four days and was very sick every month. Dorcas was named after her grandmother, who was a sorcerer. She accepted the blood of Jesus in her life and she was delivered from the powers of darkness in Jesus's name.

Many spiritual or physical things happen to kids as they grow with or without the knowledge of their parents. Witches in the family especially grandparents can manipulate grandchildren to perform rituals of witchcraft without the knowledge of their parents.

Spiritual attacks are scary to talk about, and it's too hard to explain because of confusion. There is hope in the Lord; God can set you free from the bondage of sins in Jesus's name. The blood of Jesus is the medicine for witchcraft-oriented problems. God has given you power to decide what you want to be in your life. God uses the spirit of a man to convey his message to his people in different ways. A man can be used of God or satan to accomplish missions in either way, but the good news is that God has given humankind a second chance in life. Your tomorrow is your decision today.

A child is like a seedling that must be watered with good morals and protected from any kind of evil every day. Many kids have been left by their parents like orphans with maidservants who are like demons. It is good to be busy in life, but let us set apart family time because our kids need us. It is not wise to trust a stranger with our own children 100 percent. I am talking about mothers because they feel the pain of having a child more than their husbands. We hold our wives from labor wards to delivery rooms to cheer them up, but we can't feel the pain like them. Mothers are most affected when kids are not doing well in life because everybody puts the blame on them. The touch of a mother is different in the life of her children. A son or a daughter can tell his or her mother the deepest secret no one knows. Almost everyone has more confidence with his or her mother than with any other relative.

The harsh attitude of many of us fathers has broken the close fellowship that should be between us and our kids. Taking your child to be ordained by a pastor after birth is building a wall of protection around them spiritually. The strength of a child depends on the deliverance of his or her mother. Children who have a Sunday school foundation about the Word of God cannot be stolen by the devil easily as they grow because they know what the Bible says.

I remember Tabitha, a friend of my sister, who used to come to me asking for prayers. She was tired of chasing after men who never stayed because most of them were married. She was so frustrated because wherever she went to see the witch doctors for rituals, they demanded sex first for her wishes to be granted. One day, her colleague told her that a famous herbalist was in town from Tanzania (an African nation). He was known to be a specialist in witchcraft. She booked an appointment and hurried to the hotel where he was meeting with his clients.

The witch doctor ordered her to strip naked and lie down on the bed, ready to serve idols. He came to her with a long horn, carrying a big python he had named Horny, which "burned with lust and desire." Tabitha screamed loudly, calling the name of Jesus. The witch doctor was annoyed; why did she call the name of Jesus? He said she messed up his work and Jesus couldn't hear her because she came seeking help from satan. He ordered the snake to return back to the horn and let her leave the hotel room naked, carrying her clothes to the nearest restroom.

When she went back to her house, she noticed her son got scared and started crying because she was demon-possessed already. Tabitha later came to me for prayer. I prayed for her, and she and her son were set free from bondage in Jesus's name. When she reached her house, her son hugged her and was happy like before.

Whatever you are passing through in your social life, don't give up your faith in God. "Now faith is confidence in what we hope for and assurance about what we do not see. This is what the ancients were commended for" (Hebrews 11:1-2, NIV).

Chapter Two

People the devil can use to destroy someone's life
Maidservants and relatives

Witchcraft is real. One day I was left alone at home to prepare food for my family. My brothers and sisters had gone down to the farm to prepare land for planting. A witch in my extended family came carrying a bag with some millet into my house because she knew my mother was not home. I welcomed her into my house with respect, like any other relative, because I did not know she was a witch. (I was in the third grade then.) She placed the bag of millet on my head. She ordered me to make several trips from my house to the store while walking behind me. She told me to get some millet from the bag and eat. I didn't see when she went away because she stayed behind me as she was performing her rituals of witchcraft. My stomach started aching, and I didn't remember what happened anymore. I was sick and never went to school for one year. I could see spiritual things that no one could see, like snakes and other things tormenting me in the physical. I was so weak because I vomited anything I ate and had sleepless days and nights for a year. We went from one clinic to another for medication, but every day I was worse. My mother was not a Christian then, and the only option she had was to take me to the witch doctor. When people have no light of salvation they seek help from witch doctors for cleansing rituals, per their traditions.

As the witch doctor was doing her rituals to me in a dark hut while seated on a tortoise, the memory of what happened came back to me. She said every step I took and the type of witchcraft used. She mixed the dust from a bark of a tree with porridge made of millet and told me to drink. I got delivered instantly and joined my mother, who was seated outside the hut. God gave me the strength to walk to my house by myself because my mother had carried me on her back to the witch doctor's house. God hears the cry of people in different ways, and he helps them unconditionally regardless of darkness covering their lives spiritually.

I can't say a witch doctor healed me, but God remembered me and respected the faith of my mother because we were both innocent. As I reached home, the sorcerer who had bewitched me came immediately to check on me. I told her that God healed me in Jesus's name. She didn't talk much because her witchcraft magic powers made her fail at her satanic mission to kill me. My mother, who had some wisdom, told me to forgive her, and we continued with life like nothing had happened. "Do not seek revenge or bear a grudge against anyone among your people, but love your neighbor as yourself. I am the Lord" (Leviticus 19:18, NIV).

A classmate of my elder sister used to accompany her to our house every evening after school on a purpose. She molested me sexually in secret without the knowledge of my sister. I used to run and hide anytime I saw them coming from a distance. I found it hard to explain to someone what I was enduring in secret because it was shameful and no one would believe me.

She kissed me and invaded my privacy by force. She put me under her thighs, pretending that she was playing with me any time we were caught by my elder sister. Teenage girls seduced me whenever I met with them in the neighborhood. I kept avoiding them because I was just a kid. The spirit of immorality followed me for many years. When I became of age, younger and older women liked me even when I didn't have feelings for them. A demonic spirit of immorality can possess anybody at whatever age because sex is spiritual. It is only the blood of Jesus which can set someone free from the bondage of immorality in Jesus's name. Maidservants romance with little kids possessing them with demons spirits of immorality.

As parent, we have to correct any bad behavior we notice with our kids as they grow. At times we punish our kids to correct them, but we can't kill demonic spirits in their spiritual worlds. A child is like an angel, and anyone who comes his or her way is like a friend. The only friends to little kids as they grow are their family members and maidservants. Being a parent is a great honor God has given us in our time. Monitoring the behavior of kids as they grow in our families is a full-time job for every parent.

Media and the bigger community crisis catching up with kids

"Listen, my son, accept what I say, and the years of your life will be many. I instruct you in the way of wisdom and lead you along straight paths. When you walk, your steps will not be hampered; when you run, you will not stumble. Hold on to instruction, do not let it go; guard it well, for it is your life" (Proverbs 4:10-13, NIV).

When kids are under the age of ten, the devil tries harder than ever to destroy their lives using his satanic ways. This is when children need spiritual nourishment to build their spiritual foundation in Jesus's name. Kids are anxious to learn many things within their surroundings. They start following romantic movies, which trigger their feelings and cause them to practice masturbation very early in life. The devil can use anybody to defile a child who is possessed with demonic spirits of immorality. A young girl knows how to dress by copying females in her house. Peer groups cannot influence your daughter much if you have taught her how to dress decently.

When a woman walks around half-naked, she arrests the minds of men who look at her lustfully because sex is spiritual. Dressing is the manifestation of morality or immorality in your spirit. You have to pay close attention to how you dress so that your daughter understands why she should cover her body. Make her understand with love why she should cover her body and not allow anybody to access her privacy. Rape scenarios are confusing. No one can ever imagine a close relative or a father defiling his own daughter. Teenagers kissing in secret or publicly claiming they are independent to make their own choices is a moral decay. When the devil wants parents to suffer emotionally, he attacks their kids. The Holy Spirit of God will rescue your sons and daughters from the hands of the enemy in Jesus's name.

A father should not be closer to his teenage daughter than his wife socially. There must be limitations between fathers and daughters in every society. There is no assumption when it comes to the things that can arouse lust and passion. Anything good or bad started somewhere, and it was started by somebody. Where there is a smoke, someone lit the fire.

Don't compromise a weird behavior you may notice with your son or daughter today. Some days it will be a bombshell that destroys his or her life. It is hard for a man or woman obsessed with masturbation to be a faithful husband or wife in a marriage. A woman masturbating using vibrators can't get sexual satisfaction in her marriage because of being used to electrical power. Getting used to your spouse only is very healthy in a marriage. It is our responsibilities as parents to rise up by faith and fight for our sons and daughters on our knees in Jesus's name.

Many teenagers around the world commit suicide to end their miserable lives because of drugs and sexually transmitted diseases. The devil can destroy the whole family within a very short time given the chance. Trust in God always through whatever troubles you might be enduring as a family. Encourage your kids every day to face life with confidence and hope in Jesus's name. Life is a very long journey, and people need to walk together, holding hands, as a family. We don't have to kill our sons or daughters because of making mistakes in their lives. Our daughters and their babies need our love and care because chasing them away from home is not a solution.

When a parent takes his or her daughter for an abortion, they are destroying her life. The majority of married women lost their virginity while teenagers to men who never married them. The majority of married women and single mothers have had more than one abortion. Many married couples have made the decision to kill a number of babies in unwanted pregnancies. A woman who has kept abortion secrets can't get peace in her life. The dead spirit of the baby she killed torments her every night spiritually. It is good to reveal dark secrets in your life to your spiritual leaders so they can pray for you in Jesus's name. The blood of Jesus is the only source of peace.

As a parent, we should not laugh at our neighbor's sons and daughters who have problems with drugs. We have to pray for them as we pray for ours, too. We don't know what may happen to our kids tomorrow because what goes around comes around. Parents should stop punishing their sons and daughters who have drug addictions. We can't whip a demonic spirit. Parents get worried when their kids are not doing very well in life. It is not easy to forgive and forget the pain caused by your sons and daughters. As a parent, you have to forgive them in Jesus's name. God will heal your family and restore everything with time in Jesus's name. Generational curses have no power in your life in Jesus's name. The blood of Jesus speaks better things than the blood of Abel.

Chapter Three

A child is a great nation

"Do not be yoked together with unbelievers. For what do righteousness and wickedness have in common? Or what fellowship can light have with darkness?" (2 Corinthians 6:14, NIV).

When I was young in salvation, I met this lady I loved so much. We tried to keep the relationship going, but situations separated us. After a year, she came back to me and was one month pregnant with another man's baby. She asked me to make the decision whether to abort the baby or not. When I asked her about the father of the baby, she didn't want to talk about it and told me not to say anything to anybody about it. I said, "Well, let the baby live," and she was happy because she didn't want to lose her baby, too.

I continued visiting her as her pregnancy progressed, encouraging her as a friend. I tried to keep the promise to stand with her, but somehow my relative knew the baby wasn't mine because she was my friend. When she understood that people knew we were just friends, she was not happy. When the baby was born, I went to see her in the maternity ward, and she said she was sorry. When the son was two years old, I clearly told her I didn't hate her because of her son but we were not meant to be together no matter how we pushed things to happen. I was a born again Christian, and she was not. What I called a sin was fun to her. The Holy Spirit of God rebuked both of us in a dream at the same time, and we parted ways for good. I prayed for her and said she would find a man who would love her and her son in Jesus's name. She got married to a man I knew, and she is happy in her marriage. Don't deny a child the right to live in Jesus's name.

A baby is a baby either born at white house or in the bushes. Every expectant mother must wait nine months for her baby to be born. Going for bedrest before delivery or being caught up with labor pains on your way to the hospital is all being careful. Expectant mothers of all walks of life undergo the same labor pains regardless of preparations made by their families. A rich family can use a family car to take the mother and baby home. A woman from a poor family can give birth alone in the jungle far away from home. She can trek miles to her house on a rainy, cold evening because she has no better option. When a woman from a rich family is receiving gifts from family and friends, a woman from a poor family is trekking on a muddy path with a crying baby, tired and weak.

African children face many challenges from birth to adulthood because of extreme poverty and traditions. Kids are dedicated to satan before birth because of their traditions and cultures. What you believe in becomes your god spiritually. It is only the Holy Spirit of God who can set someone free from the bondage of witchcraft in Jesus's name. Many people around the world believe in the power of charms for protection. A child of an unbeliever is surrounded by tough situations physically because his or her spiritual world is tight. Mothers from poor families leave their crying weeks- or months-old babies with other children who can't carry or feed them and go out looking for food for the whole family. A wet baby can cry for hours without help from a scorching sun. A child of three years can carry a gourd full of water from the river either alone or with the rest barefoot on a shiny day. Parents force their sons and daughters to join peer groups even when they don't want to. Even when they are tortured during rituals, they say nothing because their parents underwent the same thing. God gives his people grace to grow without medication and nutrition in many countries around the world.

Spiritual war between traditions and Christianity

My mother asked me jokingly whether I could face the traditional surgeon, and I said yes. I thought she wasn't serious because I was only twelve years old. I went downtown to graze the cattle because the schools were closed. When I heard the sound of a horn and the shouting of wild warriors, I knew I was done. The caretaker came for me, jumping up and down, singing traditional songs to give me the breaking news. Because I couldn't do otherwise, I got excited like I was prepared for the ceremony while I was actually broken in my spirit. My world changed, and everything was tasteless in my mouth. The night was too long for me. Fears of the unknown loomed in every corner of my world. I asked my mother about the seriousness of the ceremony, and she said it was for real. She told me, "You will face the monster tomorrow, and you will have a little scratch on your skin. It will be a matter of seconds but very scary." A spirit of endurance came into my heart as she was encouraging me.

Early in the morning I was the first to meet the traditional surgeon. I was the youngest and best candidate in that group because the strong words from my mother gave me victory. Spoken words are like storms because they can build you up or destroy you. Come what may, encourage somebody in Jesus's name.

Back in the day, a teenager fought between two worlds. Either he would go to school and get the light of education or remain in darkness of his or her traditions. Christian families transformed our lives in our societies because we wanted to be like them. We were loaded with much work at home because most parents didn't want their kids to go to school. It was a cold war between traditional conservatives and Christian reformists in local levels. Children of Christians often compromised their family values and joined traditionalists because of incitements from friends and relatives. Children of unbelieves became great crusaders after receiving the light of education and the Word of God.

Traditional and Christian families were totally different because of what they believed in. Children of a mother brewing alcohol became drunkards and prostitutes because they hung around with the wrong people. Living with a witch in the same family, the possibility of being bewitched is too high because of close fellowships. You can't detect a sorcerer by looking at him or her physically. Whatever people undergo in the physical is the manipulations of demonic spirits in their spiritual worlds. It is only the blood of Jesus that can open his people's spiritual eyes and help them to understand spiritual things in their lives.

Tradition is the enemy of development, education, and salvation. Traditionalists used to curse young ladies who violated their orders. Their family members could take them to the witch doctor for cleansing. Witch doctors used to molest young women sexually as part of their rituals. Witch doctors possessed them with fear to hold them hostage and ensure they remained mistresses or wives for life using dark powers of witchcraft. A witch doctor would tell a young woman she would never get happiness in life, never have sex with any human being. And finally, they would convince her to confess satan in her life. Becoming a witch is a long journey of frustration. No one can wake up and decide to be a witch, but situations and satanic rituals make one bitter. It is only God who can set one free from the bondage of witchcraft in Jesus's name.

Circumcision rituals and satanism

I endured pain for several minutes without moving my body or making noise. The whole process hardened my heart as

I was trying to build my personality and protect the family name traditionally. Initiates who moved their bodies or cried during the process were treated like outcasts. My smile was stolen from me in April of 1987, when I was circumcised, and came back again in July of 1998, when I got born again. When you become a born again Christian, the old you dies spiritually and the new you comes to live again by the grace of God in Jesus's name.

Literature that can erase the smile on your face and possess you with bitterness is from the dark world. Whoever underwent traditional circumcision ceremonies made a covenant with the dark world because blood was involved. Warriors bullied and scared initiates with crude weapons as they shaved their hair anyhow. Witches used to take an initiate's hair in that confusion for witchcraft rituals. A father marking the forehead of his son or daughter with a white powder before facing the knife was dedicating him or her to the satanic kingdom.

Going to the river naked and washing the private parts was another ritual. A traditional surgeon went around the field six times in the darkness with his team of witches, performing rituals to possess that territory before the day. A traditional surgeon circumcised a goat first and did his wicked rituals the night before circumcision ceremony. Any singing and dancing associated with the occasion was wicked and weird. To start the ritual, they sprinkled honey and milk on the initiate. There was no trace of blood or flesh seen on the field after the circumcision ceremony was over. In my community it was believed that after the circumcision ceremony, blood and flesh from initiates was taken spiritually by demon spirits, or physically by sorcerers.

A traditional surgeon would return after the operation to mark the initiates with white powder and take his payment in order to complete the ritual. If initiates refused to be marked, he could not take the money from their parents. After the circumcision ceremony was over, the brainwashing and beating of the initiate would begin. During this time, the devil made sure he deleted good morals from the initiates through these torturing rituals. Seniors taught initiates the tactic of raping women because to them sex was their right per their culture. They told initiates a warrior is the one who robs a bank, cannot be governed by a woman, never says sorry to anybody, and many other radical ideologies which would cause them great problems in the future.

The initiates disobeyed their parents and teachers immediately following the ritual. The majority of the initiates dropped out of school because of the outdated traditional culture. Girls who underwent female genital mutilation rituals were advised by their seniors never to satisfy their husbands sexually when they got married. Seniors told them that a clever woman is the one who says no to a man when she means yes. Seniors also told initiates during initiation ceremonies that a wise woman is the one who keeps secrets to herself and many other evil things. Their faces looked sad because the ritual radicalized them emotionally and physically. Because of being brainwashed by culture, the initiates were no longer innocent boys and girls, but arrogant, bitter bullies. The Holy Spirit of God can rescue anybody from the satanic kingdom in Jesus's mighty name.

The devil possesses people spiritually with demonic spirits of rejection and prostitution without their knowledge. It is not normal for a mature man in his fifties to have many lovers and refuse to marry and settle down socially. You can have a first-class honors degree and be jobless for decades because of generational curses of rejection. Someone's son or daughter can have a good job and later die of diseases or road accidents because of drunkenness. Someone's son or daughter can be left by his or her fiancée a few days before his or her wedding day because of generational curses of rejection.

Someone's son or daughter may marry and break his or her marriage within months or years because the husband was impotent or the wife could not have babies in her marriage. Someone's son or daughter may go to school and fail to read numbers or letters written on the blackboard because of diseases or possession by the demonic spirit of witchcraft, which causes blindness. Some spiritual things are hard to understand because they are beyond our knowledge. Someone's daughter may complain spiritual beings are raping her in her dreams. People may make fun of her nightmares because they are spiritually blind. A young or old man may complain of somebody taking his semen in his dreams. People can laugh at him because it is beyond their knowledge. Spiritual things are complicated to explain and confusing to understand if someone is not in the Spirit of God.

A daughter may tell her mother that spiritual babies are sacking her breast. The mother may tell her happily that she will be a mother of many kids. You can't blame her mother because it was beyond her knowledge. Having babies in your dreams is the spirit of barrenness spiritually. A daughter can tell her mother that she is having sex with or romancing a woman in her dreams. Her mother can make fun about it or rebuke her. A woman having an intimate relationship with another woman in her dreams is the spirit of lesbianism. A woman giving birth in her dreams spiritually represents the generational curses of barrenness and rejection.

Spiritual things are stronger than physical things. Whatever you went through in your life is history now. The Holy Spirit of God was with you in these situations. The devil tries to steal, destroy, or kill us every day, but God can't allow that to happen because we are his beloved sons and daughters. God monitors our steps every day although we can't see him physically. "And Jesus grew in wisdom and stature, and in favor with God and man" (Luke 2:52, NIV).

Chapter Four

The bond between relationships and marriages

"Her children arise and call her blessed; her husband also, and he praises her: 'Many women do noble things, but you surpass them all.' Charm is deceptive, and beauty is fleeting; but a woman who fears the Lord is to be praised. Honor her for all that her hands have done, and let her works bring her praise at the city gate" (Proverbs 31:28-31, NIV).

Before getting born again, I had many girlfriends in my life. I remember things we shared together, although not for love. I wasted time on old lovers who waited for me in the hope that one day we would marry and be a couple. I loved and cherished some women in my life, but they got married and left me behind. The day I met my wife, I felt like I had never met another woman in my whole life.

Relationships are stronger than friendships. Someone can have as many friends as possible, but it is rare to have two relationships the same time. A relative can introduce a man or a woman to you who later becomes your husband or wife. You can join a new church, a company, or a learning institute and meet a person who later becomes your husband or wife. Having feelings for someone is God-given. Communication, commitment, and contentment are important complements for a healthy relationship. Having a real relationship is the beginning of spiritual warfare with satan and people. The Holy Spirit of God comes into your relationship after you play your role. The voice of the Holy spirit of God comes to rebuke you or to give you the go-ahead in your relationship because he is not an author of confusion.

What is diverting and delaying spirits in a relationship?

I wanted to marry when I was in my early twenties, but I could not because I had no source of income. I ran away from beautiful women who admired me because I knew I could not keep them for long. I went away from home hoping things would be better, but situations became worse year after year. I kept strong, saying one day things would be better by faith in Jesus's name.

Things started becoming better when I became a born again Christian. Every mature person needs someone to share with him or her things of the heart as a married couple. It is hard to know by looking outside of a man or woman who is demon-possessed and who is not. Human beings speak, walk, and dress the same, although their spiritual worlds are different. Someone can be followed by demonic spirits of rejection without his or her knowledge for many years. There are so many spiritual stumbling blocks to your blessings. For you to receive your allotted inheritance that God has already released in your spirit, you have to pray hard for divine intervention in Jesus's name.

It is only God who can set a captive free from satanic bondage using his anointed servant in Jesus's name. The following are few examples of diverting and delaying spirits. Stopping education after a loss or accident, being jobless, taking too long to settle socially, or being barren in a marriage. Spiritual beings marry men and women spiritually and force them to break their relationships and marriages physically by using dark powers of witchcraft.

Keeping secrets of demonic challenges is like committing suicide. You are the only one who can speak out to your pastor and get help spiritually in Jesus's name. Yes, I know demonic spirits may threaten someone either spiritually or physically. But who don't you value much in your life—is it God or satan? Are you tired of satanic orders? Do you remember making a covenant with satan knowingly or unknowingly? Do you know how the satanic kingdom uses you? Where are they taking you in your dreams? Are you ready to confess the blood of Jesus in your life? I know it is complicated to explain what happened either spiritually or physically. Witches or demons can take someone to the bottom of the sea spiritually. Spiritual beings give many people wedding rings for marriage. There is always a way out of satanic bondage if you are willing. Reveal to all what you know about the satanic kingdom, and receive your deliverance in Jesus's name.

The devil enslaves people with demonic spirits of witchcraft, masturbation, homosexuality, and many other things to possess their lives with sadness. A young girl can be raped and later become pregnant. The parents can force her to abort the baby because of school or if the pregnancy belonged to her close relative. An evil spirit can tell a young woman she is a prostitute and she will never get married. Evil spirits can force a woman to go out at nights hunting for men to rape her so she may get peace to sleep. Someone may feel a hand blocking her private part in her dreams and hear a voice saying she will never have babies if she is lucky enough to get married. A pregnant woman may see herself giving birth in her dreams and hear voices telling her she will miscarry or have a still birth. The queen of the sea possesses women with demonic spirits to get her to like other women. The devil uses many ways to possess people with demonic spirits of confusion socially. It is only the power of confession that can set one free from satanic bondage in Jesus's name.

Reasons devil uses to delay or divert relationships

When I was in my early thirties, I cried and asked God, "For how long will I remain single?" I had severed many relationships with girlfriends because of reasons I could not understand. God used good people to rebuke me when I was in the wrong relationships, but listening was hard. When I came to salvation, Spirit-filled pastors and the Holy Spirit of God warned me, but I didn't listen. Refusing to give up can delay you socially. There is nothing better than to love and to be loved in this world. Lovers sacrifice many things for love. Everyone wishes to be happy with their spouses as long as they live. There is nothing that hurts more than separation in a relationship. Divorce is evil because it leaves someone with permanent scars.

When someone is bitter, they can curse former fiancée with words like "he or she will never be happy with any man or woman in his or her life," "he or she will never get kids to call him or her dad or mom," or "he will never make a woman pregnant." They may say these things and other threatening statements because of resentment. Likewise, someone can tie himself or herself spiritually by making promises to his or her lover in a relationship such as "he or she will never leave him or her forever," "he or she can't love any man or woman," or "he or she will never have babies with any other man or woman in life."

Lovers make covenants that strike back spiritually in case they separate or divorce. Destroying or burning an old lover's pictures, letters, and other gifts becomes spiritual witchcraft. Intimate things, such as removing clothes, become spiritual witchcraft after you separate because it is not easy to see each other naked. It is not easy to see or touch a woman's breast. It is not easy to see ladies' thighs. Taking a woman's virginity, which she had protected for many years, becomes spiritual witchcraft after separation. She can say you will never see the nakedness of another woman in your life because of bitterness. Her bitter spirit follows the spirit of her former boyfriend, making sure he is not happy socially. It is very hard to see a man crying over a woman he loves. Whenever a man sees his former fiancée with another man, he feels like he is dead. The first man who takes a woman's virginity remains her husband spiritually until that covenant is broken in Jesus's name. Why am I saying this? Both single and married women keep talking about the first day they met their lovers many years ago. It takes long to start another relationship after breaking one. Try as you can to keep your relationship and marriage in Jesus's name.

Guys who have many lovers are molested sexually in the spiritual without the knowledge of their spouses in the physical. Old lovers—either single or married—become secret lovers again after many years of separation. A married man can leave his beautiful family and go to live with a single mother because of the vows he made to her many years ago. Many married people have secret lovers known only by themselves and satan. When these old lovers meet secretly, they feel for each other like they did when they were in primary school.

Love stories are confusing and frustrating because of diseases and crimes involved. Prophets of doom have misled many people looking for their life partner because of desperation. People will pay any price to whoever can help him or her get a man or a woman he or she loves. Don't allow secret admirers to confuse you with their counterfeits. If God spoke to him, He can speak to her too because he is not an author of confusion. Don't allow false prophets to molest you sexually with their lies because God said nothing. Listen to the Holy Spirit of God more than to lies from people. Don't allow a person in your fellowship to confuse you socially because the devil can use any vehicle.

It is easier to enter into a relationship than to break it. A nagging woman can get any man she wants by using her evil ways. Men behave like little kids in the hands of immoral women. Witches possess people with demonic spirits of rejection, breaking their relationships and marriages without their knowledge. The Holy Spirit of God can enable someone to meet Miss or Mr. Right without much trouble. Trusting God is not like waiting for people's decisions.

Sue was not a happy woman, although she was a millionaire. She divorced a husband and went abroad. She left her two daughters with relatives like they were orphans. She came back home after seven years and started using her money to chase after younger men. Her social class could not allow her to go back to her drunkard husband in the village. She was no longer young enough to be married again. She used money to get a love potion to break the marriages of men she wanted, but she still remained desperate. She dressed and behaved like a teenager, but you can't hide your age, no matter how well you apply make-up. Neighbors were not able to differentiate between her lovers and boyfriends of her grown-up daughters. She used her money to catch pastors who were in need, making them her secret lovers. She removed all the witchcraft of materials she had in her house, and I destroyed them in Jesus's name. I prayed for her and went my way.

Don't hurry to divorce, but give your marriage a second chance in Jesus's name. Peace in your heart is more than money. You can't buy happiness with money.

Chapter Five

Wedding happiness and an ugly demon of divorce

We tried to stop a family member from marrying her fiancé, as he was a wolf in sheep's clothing, but she would not listen. We supported her marriage because we wanted her to be happy. Many things happened within eight months of her marriage. She tried to stay strong with her husband, but she could not endure anymore. She escaped from him with only the clothes she was wearing. She told us she didn't know she married a monster. She didn't want to discuss anything with anybody about her ex-husband. She told her pastor and her best couple friends that it was over between her and her husband. We didn't continue with more dialogues about her and the husband because she had the final word about her marriage. You can't force someone to stay in an abusive relationship or marriage. Everyone has the freedom to decide what is best for him or her. She went back to college and continued with her life. "Therefore what God has joined together, let no one separate" (Mark 10:9, NIV).

Marriage is a breakthrough achieved after battling with immorality and rejection for many years. Marriage is like an institution where all departments must discuss losses and profits together. They must settle their differences amicably with one accord and in one spirit to achieve their future goals in life. Marriage is a lifetime commitment as long as your spouse is alive. We accept each other's weaknesses in marriage every day to keep families together no matter what.

You can decide to run or hide from bad guys because you can see them but you can't do that with spiritual enemies. It is only God who can fight spiritual battles in our lives in Jesus's name because he is all-powerful.

People may do things because of ignorance or spiritual blindness becoming spiritual weapons later in life. Again, someone can be followed spiritually by generational curses of rejection without realizing it, which may make him or her get bored or stressed in marriage. Demonic spirits can make a husband or a wife to have no feelings for his or her spouse in a marriage, which may lead to divorce. Demonic spirits can cause confusion in a married woman's menses immediately after marriage. Her husband can threaten her with divorce papers because she can't conceive babies. A newly married man can have low libido, and his miserable wife can threaten to divorce him because that was not what she wanted in a man.

A married woman may worry about her husband sleeping in the living room. She may claim to have heard scary voices in the bedroom anytime he approached her sexually, which made her think he was cheating on her. She may get more confused because he always makes love with a spiritual woman in his dreams, calling her by her name. When he wakes up, he can't understand or explain what was happening in his dreams. The devil wakes her up to hear the husband enjoying sex in his dreams, and he can't get erect in the physical. A married couple can long for sex during the day, but the moment they go to bed, they are both raped by spiritual beings until the following day.

A spiritual wizard pouring cold water on the beddings in the spiritual world is the spiritual witchcraft that possesses married couples with demonic spirits of rejection. A witch approached a young lady secretly and advised her to drop school and marry her son, who was twice her age. When she said no, the witch got mad and told her she would never get married to anyone but demons. The young lady laughed and walked away because she thought the old lady was just kidding. Spoken words are like storms because people keep remembering them years later.

A teenager in high school can be raped in her dreams and later have sex with her boyfriend and get pregnant. Her mother may decide to take her for an abortion. The dead spirit of the baby she aborted will torment her in her dreams, telling her she will never have other babies in her life. A married woman can see herself in a party at the bottom of the sea. A spiritual man can give a woman a wedding ring and started making love with her in her dreams after some months. A woman can start hating her husband from the moment she got a spiritual man in her dreams. A married man can see himself having sex in his dreams. The following day, he will complain about his wife's face being as old as his grandmother.

Whatever satanic torments you might be passing through in your life, Jesus cares for you. He died for you to get delivered by his blood of redemption. There is power in confession. Unleash yourself by saying what you are passing through spiritually to your pastors, and you will be freed in Jesus's name. Relationships and marriages will stand by the grace of God.

Gifts given during a wedding day becoming a spiritual attack later

Worried, Alice came secretly to me asking for prayer because she was tired of witchcraft. She had been introduced to witchcraft by her grandmother. She revealed to me how she ruined many relationships and marriages using her witchcraft magic powers. She told me witches take money and other gifts for witchcraft rituals before giving them to the bride and bride groom during their wedding ceremony. I prayed for her, and she got delivered in Jesus's mighty name.

No one can ever believe a relative or friend can destroy his or her marriage by using witchcraft magic powers. The impact of what is said by witches on the gifts strikes marriages spiritually without the knowledge of the newly married couple. A wicked word spoken by your enemies upon your life is witchcraft. It is hard to know what witches said about your marriage after receiving money or other gifts from them.

Spiritual witches can speak destruction, using their witchcraft dark powers to cause an accident on your wedding day. Witches speak to cause confusion and stop the wedding. It is very hard to discern these spiritual witches because of the excitement on their faces and their strange movements from one location to another. Wizards are the first people to sit down at the high table very close to the bride and bride groom. They can touch, shake hands, hug, or kiss either the bride or bridegroom and release powers of witchcraft to them without anyone's knowledge. You won't listen to anybody telling you about the witch seated next to you on your big day.

Witches behave like angels when pursuing their witchcraft missions. The excitement of relatives and friends may make couples think that everyone who attended their wedding ceremony was happy for them. You may know witches from your own community but not from your fiancée's side. Your best friend may be a best friend of your worst enemy. People of the inner circle might be witches, and there is no way you can stop them from attending your big day.

A witch values his or her idols more than anything of this world. A sorcerer can kill anybody—regardless of their relationship to the person—in order to appease his or her demonic spirits of witchcraft. It is very hard to know who brought suffering in your marriage immediately after your honeymoon. What are these sufferings? What secrets do you know in your dreams? What can you see and hear in the spiritual world? Do you trust God in your suffering, or do you doubt him? Have you ever acknowledged Christ Jesus as the Lord and Savior in your life? The Holy Spirit of God can rescue your marriage from the bondage of witchcraft in Jesus's name.

I know you have never conceived in your marriage for years. I know it is hard to forgive a witch who made you lose a baby of two months. God will restore love in your marriage again in Jesus's name. I know no one can understand what happened after you use beddings you were given by your best friend on your wedding day. I know it is hard to accept that your best friend was the old girlfriend of your husband. Witches take the clothes of married couples to the witch doctor for rituals to make them separate.

Demonic spirits can order a married woman spiritually to kill, poison, or pursue other men out of wedlock. One text message from a witch— using her dark powers of witchcraft—can break a happy marriage. Witches possess married couples with demonic spirits of rejection and immorality to break their marriage. The solution of witchcraft-oriented torments is the blood of Jesus. Whatever it is, take everything to God in prayer. God, who enabled you to meet with your spouse, will keep your marriage in Jesus's name.

A grandmother may convince her granddaughter that she is supposed to miscarry two times in her marriage before having babies because it has been a covenant in their family for many generations. Families who are not Christian have many dark secrets known only by them. The blood of Jesus has the power to break generational curses.

Traditionalists used to curse individuals who refused to comply with their orders in various communities, especially in Africa. Problems associated with a curse or witchcraft, can't be solved or treated with earthly medication because things of the spirit are more powerful than the physical things. It is only the blood of Jesus which can deliver someone from the powers of darkness in Jesus's name.

If you are bewitched, you can't get a diagnosis of any disease—or the medication to take—because the laboratory results are always negative. A Christian woman in a troubled marriage may be tempted to visit a witch doctor. Married women cheat in their marriage because of desperation for babies. The majority of them get sexually transmitted diseases or lose their marriage because of unfaithfulness. Your former girlfriend may give you a gift to take to your wife because she wasn't able to attend the wedding. And after some days, you may start hating your wife because of the power of witchcraft. Snakes may make love with women in their dreams, possessing them with demonic spirits of rejection.

There are so many things the devil can use to make people's lives miserable. It is only the blood of Jesus that can calm down storms in our marriages in Jesus's name. Every person in a relationship or marriage has a different story about how they survived storms by the grace of God. Those who hurried to separate or divorce will never advise you to hold on because of bitterness and condemnation.

Immoral past attacking your future happiness

After Sunday service, Moses told me to pray for him. He said he was tired of masturbating and having sex with cows in his village. He said old women had been raping him in his dreams for many years. Moses said he had been avoiding young women in his life because he had no feelings for any woman. He was in his early forties, and he didn't have a girlfriend. I prayed for him and told him God would remember him in Jesus's name. Many youths around the world are slaves to masturbation.

Demonic spirits of masturbation have destroyed many marriages. I know you may get frustrated in your marriage because your husband can't satisfy you sexually, like electric power. Practicing masturbation opens the door for spiritual beings to enter your spiritual world. A married woman can pretend she loves her husband. The truth is, she has no feelings for him. The husband can't satisfy her sexually the way a vibrator does during masturbation. Many girls become lesbians in high school and college. All lesbians are married spiritually, and they hate men in the physical. The queen of the sea possesses them with satanic power to like other women.

You have to reveal to your pastor the secrets of lesbianism that you know. There is no way spiritual beings can share a man or a woman with people of this world. When women romance each other, one of them grows male genitals spiritually and becomes the husband. There are millions of lesbians around the world who meet in various places. There is no parent who can accept that his or her daughter is a lesbian. Teenage girls who like staying alone in their rooms and away from others have many things that disturb them socially.

No parent can believe her daughter who is a Christian and a chair lady in the choir is capable of seducing other girls in the neighborhood. A parent can't accept what his or her daughter does with her girlfriends in her bedroom. Women who had many lovers in the past get bored sexually in their future marriage. Married women who were prostitutes have a hard time staying faithful to one man in a marriage.

A mother of seven who was married—as a second wife—came to me asking for prayer. She said there was a spiritual man who raped her every morning at exactly five o'clock. Any time she saw a handsome man, she wet her pants and imagined having sex with him. She had many lovers in her life because of desperation.

The mother's twin daughters had the same generational curses of immorality. Her daughter, who was in high school then, told me she had three boyfriends. She said that almost every night she dreamed of going to a nightclub under the sea, where she would wear miniskirts and dance with men. She complained about being raped by dogs almost every night in her dreams. The mother's fifteen-year-old son said three witches physically raped him every night without her knowledge. He was much confused because he didn't understand how those old witches entered his house in the physical world. He would physically make love with a witch in his house, but his mother's husband would not hear anything. During the day, the boy could not even look at them because of shame, but at night he waited to meet the witches in his house or somewhere else. The young boy looked confused. I prayed for him, and he got delivered in Jesus's mighty name. Witches never visited him again—either spiritually or physically—because a revealed secret is no longer a weapon.

The only medicine for witchcraft magic powers is the blood of Jesus. The Holy Spirit of God will deliver you from demonic spirits of masturbation in Jesus's name. Spiritual beings have no power over your life in Jesus's name. The Holy Spirit of God will restore your marriage in Jesus's name. God will bless you with babies in your marriage in Jesus's name. Your husband or wife who has gone away for months or weeks is coming back to you again in Jesus's name. I cancel every satanic covenant you made—knowingly or unknowingly—with the dark world for love in Jesus's name. God will bless you with more babies in your marriage, and the spirits of the babies you aborted will not torment you again in Jesus's name.

You can't force your son or daughter to stay in a marriage where there is no love. Being in a dead marriage is like being in a prison socially. Where there is no love in a marriage, there is no sexual satisfaction, which leads to separation because of unfaithfulness. The more lovers you had as a youth, the more problems you encounter socially in your future marriage. It is only God who can deliver somebody from sexual altars in Jesus's name.

Separation and divorce affect women socially more than men. A man can decide to marry a second wife or keep mistresses. It is very hard for a married woman to go out of wedlock. A married woman may end up getting married to the poorest man, one she hates to have in bed sexually. Most desperate men or women live in the past because they can't stand their bored spouses. They live in a world they wish they knew. Any time you see a smart married man, you know he has a well-groomed wife in the house. What makes married men get bored in their marriages? A clean woman has clean kids and a clear environment. Dirty women make their husbands run away from them in frustration. Men are like lions because they like taking the best and the freshest. A smart woman knows how to keep her husband happy regardless. Happy men always talk about their beautiful wives and kids. Ask your husband what made him love you so you can keep improving it in your marriage. Your husband is like your firstborn son.

Desperate men and women who are in forced relationships and marriages always think about their old lovers and how they can get them back. Happiness in marriage is worth more than gold and silver. The secret to a happy marriage is learning how to forgive each other unconditionally because there is no one who is perfect.

Chapter Six

Married couples must be respected by all people

Our world changed when we got married. We started being careful because it was not about us anymore. We started getting involved in many things that we never valued socially when we were single. People started respecting us in our society because we made the decision to grow. I felt loved and honored to have a woman in my life who was my wife.

Married couples are respected by everyone in every society. During the engagement period, lovers are encouraged by families and brethren to keep away from the sin of fornication. Sex before marriage had consequences in both traditional and Christian families. Sex offenders were excommunicated from the church because it was a sin of fornication.

Relationships and marriages differed from one community to another per the customs of those people. In some communities, a girl had to retain her virginity until marriage while in others, sex was a sign of maturity in women. In some communities, parents advised their sons to impregnate their girlfriends before marriage to know their fertility because every society considered barrenness a curse. The betrothal of young girls was allowed in some communities as long as the man paid a dowry to her parents per their custom. Many communities discouraged sex with young boys and girls before circumcision. If a gentile made a girl pregnant, a dowry was paid in full to the offended family, and he underwent cleansing to be accepted back into the clan again.

In my culture, romantic relationships were not allowed between lovers until the alleged fiancée gave some dowry to the girl's family to open the marriage negotiations. The family told the young man to go to his parents first to weigh the seriousness of the matter before rushing into sex. During the engagement, the young man was allowed to visit the fiancée's family. The young lady was allowed to take food to her lover and, if need be, chat for a little while in an open place. It was the responsibility of the girl's mother to make sure the young man was out of the compound in time. If the boyfriend stayed until late at night, he was given a room—far away from their daughter—to sleep in until the next day. Mothers made sure their daughters were safe. Daughters were not allowed to be too close to their fathers per the traditions of my people.

Mothers and daughters discussed social stuff like age-mates. A foolish woman could arrange secretly with her daughter how to meet her boyfriend without the knowledge of her father. A young lady could plan to meet her boyfriend and have sex without the knowledge of her parents. If ladies behave well in relationships, we can have pure weddings because no man will rape the woman he loves. Immoral women seduce men in different ways because they know their weak points. An old or young woman can risk leaving her family members in order to stay with the man she loves. The majority of mothers both in traditional and Christian families took their daughters for abortions secretly after their lovers abandoned them.

To some societies around the world, virginity was the qualification for marriage. A tribe at the Kenyan coast supervised a bride and bridegroom having sex during the marriage ceremony. Curious men and women had to see bedding with blood to prove the woman was a virgin. Mothers protected their daughters from having sex before marriage because pure weddings were the pride of the family. During the seclusion period, young women were advised by old ladies on how to handle men to avoid rape, separation, and unfaithfulness in African traditional marriages.

Women were considered potters, mentors, and teachers of their own kids while their husbands were out working to provide for them. Many married men in Africa work away from home, and must leave their wives and kids for several months at a time. The majority of retired men in Africa die early because of stress. After working all their lives to ensure their children have a bright future, these men realize when it's too late that their wives have ruined the lives of their sons and daughters. Women are like hens in our societies. They can cover their eggs (children) or decide to expose them to the air and rot. A noble woman can breed kings and princes in her family. Kids follow whatever their mothers do and speak as they grow because they spend quality time with them.

A woman can decide to give birth to a child or to abort it. Some women are kind, and others are like monsters. Few men can kill or throw a crying baby into a latrine, but the majority of single and married women can do that. Mothers can breastfeed babies or not. They can give them nutritious food or leave them hungry. They can teach them good or bad manners, and even the language they speak is called the mother tongue.

A mother knows every characteristic of every child in her family. She knows the one who will take care of her in her old age, and the one who would kill her just to get her property. Caring mothers give their kids sermons when the father is home so that both parents can discipline the disobedient son or daughter together. They do this to avoid future crises in families. When kids go the wrong way, everybody blames the mother. In traditional families, parents have a decision to make about who their sons and daughters will marry.

The parents of a young man had many questions to ask the neighbors about their intended daughter-in-law. Does she respect her parents, age-mates, and elders? Is she lazy or hardworking? Is she humbled or in a crisis? Is she a peacemaker or violent? Is she God-fearing or a witch? And many other questions about virtues that anybody would love to see in someone's life. You could not surprise your parent with a husband or a wife in traditional families without involving them from step one.

Those were the beautiful old days when caring and concerned parents discussed marriage issues. Today things have changed because of education, religion, and freedom to interact with people from various cultures and believes. Marriage is no longer a community issue but an individual decision. You can marry or remain single because it is not an offense. You can marry whomever you want from whichever tribe you choose because marriage is confidential. Young people meet from far and wide. They can decide to marry without asking for any moral guidance from their parents. You may think your parents have no right to interfere with your happiness in marriage, but they might be seeing what you can't see now.

The spirit of ignorance and loneliness have turned many women into lesbians, prostitutes, single mothers, and second wives. Divorcees marry many husbands or wives because to them it is not a sin. Their kids suffer psychologically because they can't understand why they can't see their biological fathers or mothers. Neglected kids who live with cruel stepfathers or stepmothers become drug addicts and criminals because of bitterness. These innocent kids seek refugee in their grandparents and relatives, who cannot understand their pain. The majority of these teenagers end up in jail, and others die of diseases and bullet wounds.

A traditional African girl in an engagement

In many communities in Africa, a family would use a girl as an asset. Every mature girl was allowed to marry after a female genital mutilation ceremony because that was the bridge to adulthood. Parents were allowed traditionally to ask their sons and daughters why they were taking so long to settle socially. Every parent wanted their sons and daughters to marry early and be responsible fathers and mothers. Questions such as "When are you giving us grandchildren?" or "Are you okay?" could make someone marry any man or woman who would come his or her way because of pressure. Any time a young man said he had a girlfriend, it brought happiness to everybody in the society.

The elders from the young man's side would visit his fiancée's family with gifts, asking for an early marriage. The young lady came before the elders to receive the gifts from the young man's family and accept his friendship. She was advised never to have any boyfriend because she was somebody's wife traditionally. The young man would visit his fiancée's house with his age-mate to avoid the temptations of sex.

If the young woman refused to take the gift from the elders, it was equally honored by the community. This is because no parent was allowed to force his or her daughter to marry a man she didn't love. Marriage negotiations could commence without any restriction to both families. If the young girl had not undergone female genital mutilation, the young man's family was supposed to pay an additional dowry for her to undergo that rite of passage. The dowry was supposed to be paid in full to the girl's family before the marriage ceremony.

The breaking of the engagement was allowed traditionally before the marriage ceremony if a young man's or woman's family was associated with witchcraft, unfaithfulness, or inherited diseases. Communities helped poor families pay dowries back in the day because there was not much hatred like today. Newly married couples were allowed to live independently in their own house to plan their own things as a family. Married couples were given cattle and land by the man's family.

The man was supposed to live with the wife, with or without babies. When a baby was born, the community celebrated the addition. The wife was supposed to make her husband happy and do other domestic chores in her marriage while the husband grazed cattle. The wife was supposed to make sure she attended her husband's sexual needs. Traditionally, unfaithfulness in a marriage was evil, although the man was allowed to marry as many wives as possible. Both single and married warriors spent most of the time grazing cattle and feeding themselves so they could fight their enemies back in the day. Young and old people surprised a newly married couple at their house when they weren't expected just to weigh a wife's generosity.

During the seclusion period, elderly women trained young women on how to be tough in all situations to keep their marriages intact. Their husbands went away from home for months looking for green pastures for their cattle.

A married woman was not allowed to go back to her parents after an argument with her husband because people considered that being soft. If a sister or daughter married a man who came from a poor family, her people could help her and encourage her to stay. Beating women traditionally was a sign of discipline, but to me, that was illegal and a sin. It was very hard see a married woman commit adultery, even if her husband went away from home for years.

A married man had to build his own hut a certain distance from the main house. He would meet his wife in his hut away from their kids and discuss serious family matters or have sex. Married men from my tribe believed that sharing a bed with their wives was being a slave to sex and women. I disagree with traditional conservatives because I believe marriage is for couples to stay together. When a woman was breastfeeding, she was not supposed to visit her husband's hut for sex. When the child grew big enough to carry a plate of food to his or her father, the wife was allowed to visit her husband's hut for the next baby.

African women were humbled and careful when handling their men. In many communities in Africa, a wife would choose a younger and more beautiful woman for her husband if she herself was barren, old, or diseased. Men provided food and security for their families. Young men and women interacted with other communities. They brought admirable lifestyles to their communities to liberate them. Even after receiving the light of salvation and education in many African communities, we have radical traditional conservatives because individuals have not accepted change in their hearts.

A young woman could go abroad for whatever reason and try to keep her virginity. She had to return home with her friend to ask permission from her parents to start a relationship. Nowadays marriage is not a community thing, as it was during the pre-colonial period in Africa. Youths waits for the perfect will of God in their relationships, not in the traditions of their people anymore. Youths are in great fear because of the HIV/AIDS epidemic across the whole world. Many youths have decided to be born again Christians in our communities because of a fear of the unknown. It is a great tragedy in our time to bury young and old, singles and married people because of HIV and AIDS.

"The Lord God said, 'It is not good for the man to be alone. I will make a helper suitable for him'" (Genesis 2:18, NIV). God created a woman for Adam out of his rib, and he was happy to have a companion. Husbands must love their wives the way Christ Jesus loves the church. Someone has to be saved to understand the perfect will of God in his or her relationship and marriage.

Marriage is a very big mask that you can't venture into without God. Where God is involved, there are no regrets or confusion because God is not an author of confusion. Everyone who is in a relationship has a long, interesting story on how he or she met his or her lover. The greatest task is knowing how to maintain the marriage to avoid the stress of separation. You may meet your husband or wife in the church, in college, at work, walking on the street, or at any other place. It is only God who can make you to meet the right man or woman in your life. Relationships require long-term commitment through the help of the Holy Spirit of God. The Holy Spirit of God can tell you either to go ahead or to drop it. If you are not patient in a relationship, you can lose a wonderful future husband or wife.

A relationship is a hidden treasure for you to discover

A relationship starts by having a desire to have one man or woman of your choice in your life socially. It takes a high level of faith in God for you to choose a man or a woman to be your husband or wife. Because what God does is approve or disapprove what you have chosen. God will never tell Betty that John loves you. God gives someone favor to be loved by a man or a woman he or she loves only if he or she is in his spirit.

Don't allow anybody to tell you that God has said you are his or her future husband or wife. If God spoke to him or her, he can speak to you because he is not an author of confusion. Don't accept falsehoods from your spiritual leaders about who your future husband or wife is. It is hard to disagree with someone who says God has shown him or her in a dream who will be his or her husband or wife. A dream is an inside story known only by the receiver. The majority of married couples met somewhere, not in their dreams. When you make a move in the right season, when the man or woman you love is in your hands, it is a great breakthrough socially.

As long as you have made your decision about your fiancée, don't ask anybody's opinion of him or her. Don't make fun of dreams you see about your fiancée in the spiritual world. Demonic spirits know when you are about to settle socially. Follow the directions of the Holy Spirit of God in your relationship to avoid disappointment in the future.

You will reach a point in your relationship where you have to forget about somebody's' beauty and focus on what the Holy Spirit of God says to you. If the Holy Spirit of God rebukes you to leave the man or woman you love, you have to obey him because he knows why. God can speak to someone who is in a wrong relationship any time he wants to correct him or her. No one can question God when he wants to make our crooked ways straight because he hates separation and divorce.

Never hide anything from your fiancée to avoid disappointment in the future. Never fear sharing your feelings with your fiancée in a relationship to avoid the dangers of fornication. Discuss familiar spirits in your families so you can pray together in Jesus's name. Abstain from sexual intercourse before marriage because it is a sin of fornication. You must control your feelings because you may tempt your fiancée. Avoid meeting alone in dark corners. Don't hug or kiss your fiancée if you can arouse his or her feelings because salvation will continue even after your wedding day.

You have to share your weakness with your fiancée to avoid any doubts in your relationship. You have the right to decide who to marry. If you marry someone who is not saved, you will backslide because sex is not a sin to him or her. If you fornicate, you have to inform your pastor so you may have a matrimonial ceremony instead of a holy, pure wedding. You can cheat the congregation on the altar, but you can't mock God because he knows every secret in your heart.

Ladies try to keep their relationships intact more than men do during courtship. There are God-fearing women who are not ready to fornicate before marriage. Men who are not saved and delivered will seduce their fiancées and have sex with them before marriage. It is hard to find a young man who has only had one lover in a relationship. It is possible to find a young lady who has only had one lover in her life. When it comes to the things of the heart, women take more risks than men. It is very hard to find a normal man who has never had sex before marriage. You can find ladies in their thirties and older who are still virgins and are waiting for the perfect will of God. It is very hard to find a woman who has raped her own son. We see fathers defiling their own daughters in the media.

A strong relationship depends on the character of the girlfriend. A pure wedding can only happen by the grace of God. Demonic spirits of immorality make lovers backslide in their relationships and run short of God's glory in their lives. No one wants to fornicate before marriage and run away from the church because of embarrassment. No one wants to stay alone, not get married, and not be happy like the rest of his or her age-mates. No one chooses to be a single mother. No one wishes to be a prostitute. No one wants to have a wedding while pregnant. Nobody wants to be excommunicated from the church by their pastor because of immorality. No pastor would like to stop preaching because of immorality and go back to drinking and prostitution again. You can only maintain righteousness in relationships by the grace of God.

If you hear a certain couple fornicated before their wedding day and you are not married, don't laugh at them. You don't know the opposition you will face in your future relationship. It is only God who can understand the weakness of a man. If you fornicate while in a relationship, don't take oaths in the church. You know very well that sex is a covenant and you can't be a virgin again. It is better to feel ashamed when confessing your sins than to die with condemnation and go to hell.

Hypocrites in the church may call you evil names, but never mind them because you have pleased your Creator. Your fiancée may break off your engagement, but you must be strong in the Lord. There is no loss when you follow the perfect will of God in your life. It is only God who can connect you with the right man or woman in your life.

Chapter Seven

Taking a risk by faith to get the man or the woman you love

Nothing can stop you from getting the love of your life if you are in the right season. It is only God who can direct your steps when praying for your life partner. Many people have compromised their faith in God because of confusion in their social lives. It is hard to start another relationship after breaking one. Never show the person you admire your desperation. He or she may take advantage of your situation, molest you sexually, and dampen you. Don't lose the man or woman God has brought your way. As long as you have peace with him or her, God will give you victory in Jesus's name. Don't think that men or women will be pining for your love all the time. Many youths, especially ladies, take a long time to accept proposals. The majority of young women end up missing their life partners while pursuing their dreams socially. Some dreams may take long to mature, and every day people grow old and tired. Men may live for many years as bachelors surrounded by young ladies, but women are seasonal like flowers. Once a season of a beautiful woman is over, she withers like a flower. An old man can marry a woman of his daughter's age because of riches. A man can marry a woman of any caliber for love, but it is very hard for a woman to be married to someone who has no job.

Love your partner unconditionally because today it is you, but tomorrow is in the hands of God. Provide as well as you can for your fiancée in a relationship because his or her shame is yours too. Be proud of your fiancée regardless. Remember, many things happen when someone is in need. The devil reminds people of the bad things their spouses did to them when they were struggling with poverty in their lives. No one knows about tomorrow.

Don't let the enemies of your happiness destroy your relationship. There is no time where you will marry your relatives, no matter how close you might be. You can provide for your fiancée either while near or far. Don't let your fiancée mess you up spiritually because your salvation is your personal journey. The devil can use anybody to steal your salvation. You have to value God more than your fiancée. Your fiancée can decide to leave you, but King Jesus will be there for you. Keep yourself away from anything that may lead you to sin before the Lord. There is a price to pay in every relationship.

My personal testimony about the faithfulness of God in a relationship

I met a lady—who eventually became my wife for a short time—in her neighborhood where I visited. I liked her, but I could not open up to her because I didn't have much time. Many things ringed in my mind but I kept quiet. I knew deep in my heart that she could be my wife. My brother and I had to leave no matter how I wished to hang around with her more. We exchanged contact information and started communicating.

I met her again after two weeks when the country was in hot skirmishes after the 2007 general elections in Kenya. We started our relationship without the knowledge of her people because she was working away from home in the city. I planned to visit her people the second time as a pastor in order to pray for her elder brother, who was not feeling well. Family members and friends met at her home, and I had two days of miracles, signs, and wonders in Jesus's name. She broke the news of our relationship to her father as we were leaving the compound on our way to Nairobi City. I didn't want to mix my personal issues with ministry work. I saw tension on the faces of her aunts, who had come for prayer. I didn't worry much because we had already discussed it with my wife.

We visited her family again after a couple of months because of the cold war, which was going on with her people. Most of her relatives were trying to convince her to leave me because of a difference in our cultural customs. With time, they realized our love was for real. They said I had to meet her elders so they could make a dowry decision. Although my in-laws knew traditional customs and Christian values did not agree, they still insisted I meet the elders. We agreed not to meet the elders because of our faith. I dealt with her father only because her brothers adhered to the cultural customs.

I gave him the portion of the dowry I had with the agreement to pay the rest after the wedding. I explained to him openly the financial status I was in then as a minister of God. My brothers-in-law teamed up and ordered their father to explain more about the dowry. We agreed with my wife that nothing would change our wedding date and there would be no more money for the dowry. Many changes were made to the agreements per their traditions, but nothing could stop our wedding arrangements. From my hometown to my wife's house was two days' drive. I calculated many things, but there was no way I could meet their demands due to finances, time, and distance.

When the going got tough, I asked my in-laws to hold our wedding at my wife's home church. The many questions that the pastors and elders had about me intensified because of their traditions. A local pastor from her home church rang the pastor in Nairobi City who was going to officiate the wedding. He said the wedding should stop because I didn't finish the dowry and my in-laws knew nothing about me. The pastor my wife supported single-handedly for more than eight years started asking her many questions about me: "Who ordained your fiancée to be a pastor? What is his calling? How will you raise money for the wedding without a committee and pre-wedding?" I felt bad. Although we had been in a relationship for two years and three months, we abstained from sex by the grace of God.

Finally, our wedding date was announced at my local church. My wife called her dad and told him about the wedding date and the preparations we had already made. Many questions rang in my head. If the wedding was cancelled, what would I tell my family, relatives, and friends when we had already given out wedding cards? What could my wife's work colleagues think of her? Would I have the courage to stand before the congregation and preach again? It is very frustrating when you are in the middle of mayhem and don't know what will happen. My wife was crying, asking herself questions about why her loving dad was hard on her wedding arrangements. She thought that if her mother was still alive, things could be better. Time heals all wounds, and God has his own ways of calming down the storms in our lives.

When the going gets tough, you have to be prayerful and quiet in the Lord. Silence is the best weapon. My in-laws were not the problem; the devil was trying to shake our faith in God. We forgave all our opposition in Jesus's name. My brother and my wife's sister gave us financial support to make our big day great. We had a historic wedding by the grace of God. We had a convoy of cars, a professionally decorated reception, and buffet counter packed full of food and drink for everyone. God supplied more than we could imagine. You have to support your fiancée financially if you can. At the end of the day, it will mean happiness for both of you, not just your husband. Your job, beauty, or family background can't be your husband. Don't pressure your brothers- or sons-in-law when paying the dowries; support their weddings. The man who marries your daughter—from whichever race he comes—becomes your son.

One month after our wedding, I won a green card lottery. It was a very big surprise we never expected. When my wife texted me a message saying I had won a green card lottery, I didn't scream in excitement. I felt humbled in the Lord. Good people were happy for my green card because I had tried to go abroad for more than ten years. Getting married is starting a long journey where you need God to keep you strong. It is only God who can encourage married couples to face situations in their marriage together, in Jesus's name.

Women make families stand with or without money. God has given them the power to overcome stressors in their marriage. Married women look forward by faith to having kids and happiness in future more than men. Women are like potters. They shape their kids how they want in their marriages. Wise women love their husbands unconditionally. Foolish women with long mouths keep their husbands away from home and encourage them to go to prostitutes. A prudent wife is like an angel to her husband.

Men in happy marriages keep talking about their wives and kids. They go home early to be with their wives and kids. If you can't get happiness in your family, you can't get joy anywhere. No one can love you like your husband, wife, or kids. Loving wives feed their husbands with spoons like babies. They call them magic names that make them grow younger every day because of love. Men cry tears like babies after offending their loving wives socially. Loving husbands explain to their wives how nagging women seduce them in their office. A caring woman says things to her husband like: "How was your day, sweetheart? Why the long face? Why are you looking stressed? Who offended you? Take a hot shower, and you will be all right, my love."

There is no privacy between a husband and wife because a problem discussed is a problem solved. Women who are happy in their marriages look younger every day. Stress makes women ugly, weak, and old. Caring wives teach their husbands personal grooming, giving them time to learn and accept change. Men are slow learners because of the inborn seed of ignorance. A generous woman brings blessing to her family. Givers don't give out of abundance, but giving is a spirit from God. Giving in a marriage opens the wombs of barren women. God blesses them with kids who will be a blessing to them, too. God-fearing married women are happy to see kids from other families trusting God for theirs someday. If you hate to see other peoples' babies, you will never hold a baby with your hands. "Dear friends, let us love one another, for love comes from God. Everyone who loves has been born of God and knows God" (1 John 4:7, NIV).

Chapter Eight

Marriage and challenges involved

I was a local pastor with no income when I met my wife. I had a small house I had built on my brother's property. My wife encouraged me every day with great words of hope when I was down. One of her best friends from the city kept asking her secretly, "Where is John's house? Why are you having a party in his mother's house?" For the four days we stayed with them after the wedding, she was eager to see my house. My wife told her my house was downtown and the roads were not passable because of heavy rain. She shared with me what her friend told her after five years. She knew God would give us a beautiful home someday. We owned the same property, which used to be my brother's, and built a bungalow by the grace of God.

Marriage represents a permanent relocation for a lady, as she goes to live with a new person. It is not easy for a newly married woman to start fresh with new people, new characters, and a new environment. Newly married women have to accept their new environments first because it is a lifetime commitment. A daughter of the mayor can marry a poor man from the countryside. She has to forget the limousine at her parents' house. She has to prepare to trek long distances in harsh, sunny climates in her new home. Maybe she used to eat different courses of food in her mother's house. She has to adjust and be herself in her new house. She and her husband have to join hands and work hard in their marriage.

There is nothing permanent in this world. Keep your smile even when you pass through hardships in your marriage. Don't let anything steal the love you have for your spouse. Keep trusting God for kids, and stop getting worried. Kids make women have confidence and peace in their marriage. Necessity is the mother of invention in many areas of our lives. Don't allow the enemy to destroy your marriage. You can solve your own problems as a family, trusting God for a breakthrough in Jesus's name.

It is good to get advice from friends and relatives if there is chaos in your marriage. But you have to know that the majority of these "friends" are not for real but for your downfall. Don't let anybody dominate your spouse, regardless of their relationship to him or her. Love is for only two people, not three. Men are good initially, but with time their wives make them dictators. Where there is no future, there is regret and desperation in a marriage.

Don't let your parent break your marriage by humiliating your spouse. Your spouse is your best friend in this life. Men are more aggressive than women when choosing life partners. Wise newly married women try harder to be close to their in-laws. Your kids have a loving atmosphere when you are at peace with your in-laws. A good wife will make her husband be loved by his parents.

Many teenagers commit crimes as they grow, leaving their parents' hearts bleeding. A good wife gives a husband a good name in the family and in the society. A good wife brings family members together because of her extended hospitality. A good wife will feed and take care of her father- or mother-in-law when they are sick or old. Taking care of your parents at an old age is like getting blessings from God. A good wife brings forth great kids with the right behavior. If your husband loves you in a marriage, he will love your kids, too. Men have nothing to boast about in a marriage. What makes men proud is what their wives have protected. A rude father can leave kids with no food, but a mother can't do that. Great mothers in Africa and around the world dig their farms in humility and get food for their kids. Great women accept their husbands back home after they have been away for many years. They make sure sons and daughters have forgiven them.

Men are rarely seen with their kids. Mothers keep thinking about their babies wherever they go, regardless of their commitments in life. A mother will call either a teacher or someone at home to ask about her son or daughter if they do not feel well. Very few fathers will remember to make that commitment. Most of the time women cry along the streets or in their office because they disagree with their husbands. It is very hard to hear a man telling his wife sorry even after he hurts her. Women carry and kiss pictures of their husbands and kids in their offices. Some men don't even remember how their wives and kids look like until they return back home. Married women get worried when their husbands refuse to receive phone calls. Very few men will remember to call their wives and tell them their whereabouts. Married women always worry about many things in their family. Their husbands come later to support their initiatives. Men like disagreeing with the projects of women. Men like being number ones even when they are failing in life. Stressed married women lose beauty and get older with time while their husbands get more handsome, younger, and stronger. It is only God who can keep marriages in Jesus's name.

Enemies of a happy marriage

The devil is not happy when a husband and wife are in harmony.

A woman can make her marriage stand in the midst of storms socially. Women can be stronger or weaker than men spiritually. If a woman makes a decision, she takes time to change her mind. The Bible refers to women as weak vessels.

A woman feels inferior when her husband disagrees with her on many family issues. A woman likes being number one always, even when she is wrong. There is no man in his right mind who likes fighting or insulting his wife in front of their kids and strangers. Notorious women behave like lunatics when forcing things to happen in their marriage. If married women can know how to handle social crisis, we can have peaceful marriages in our societies.

A man can't maneuver his way through things in a marriage without the support of his wife. A woman can organize her family alone, without a man by her side. You may not get everything you want in a man or a woman, but you need each other to make a family complete. Generational curses can destroy your marriage without your knowledge. No one can blame someone because of things that were beyond his or her understanding. The only way for you to know the things of the Spirit is to get saved. The Holy Spirit of God is the best teacher. You need God in your marriage. As a husband or a wife, you have a duty to do in your marriage. Some issues in a marriage are created by family members or strangers. No one knows your husband or wife more than you do. There is no one who can teach you how to live with your husband or wife more than you can.

Don't air your husband's or wife's dirty laundry to outsiders because his or her shame is yours, too. You had better get used to your husband or wife and improve him or her. You may not notice the weaknesses of your spouse early in your marriage. Lovemaking is a hidden treasure that must be protected in a marriage. People do hire guys to spy on their cheating spouses, but no results can restore trust in their marriage again.

A wise woman should not forget what made her husband ask for her friendship. Married women should ask their spouses what they like about them so they may improve it throughout their marriage. If it is your hair, don't shave. If it is your body shape, check your diet. If it is cosmetics or accessories, wear them always. If it is a model of dressing, try to maintain the standards. If it is cleanliness, take showers regularly. Stinking environments have forced many married spouses to stop enjoying sex in their marriage.

Don't kiss your husband or wife with a dirty mouth. Take your bedding to the laundry regularly. Make your bed, and spray the bedroom with nice perfumes if possible. Married couples enjoy sex together and do not make love by force like rape. Don't let anything steal the language of love in your marriage. Don't allow anybody to teach you ways to disrespect your spouse. Prepare food for your family early. Don't allow house girls or watchmen to be best friends with your spouse. Don't allow kids to steal the love you had for your spouse. Don't allow house girls to do duties of hospitality for your husband when you are home. Address the dressing code with all females living in your house.

Make sure your husband is decently dressed before going out. Make sure everything and everybody is clean. Make sure the living room is always clean. Avoid sitting down carelessly and exposing your private parts. Stop breastfeeding your baby openly in public. Even if you are breastfeeding, make sure you and the baby are clean. Lack of personal grooming in marriage makes your feelings for each other deflate slowly like a balloon.

Don't trust your closest family friends and relatives with your husband. Welcome everyone in your family, but protect your husband as much as you can. Once he is taken away from you, you will have a hard time getting him back again. He can't be the same father of your kids you knew for many years. Don't allow your husband to hang around for hours with relatives. You need time together to discuss family issues before you sleep. Mothers-in-law are so possessive and jealous of their sons when they realize how close they are to their wives and kids.

Mothers-in-law call their sons between meals, almost as if you never cook meals for your husband. In-laws badmouth their daughter-in-law to their son to make sure she goes away. No one can agree that his or her mother is a witch. Mothers-in-law refer to their daughters-in-law as women because of hatred. Your mother-in-law can tell your husband how she longs to have grandchildren if you have refused to conceive babies. She can exaggerate her son's physical changes. She can even advise him to marry another woman who can cook for him properly and give him sons and daughters.

Evil mothers-in-law can lie about their daughters-in-law having love affairs out of wedlock. Very few mothers will support their sons and daughters-in-laws in order to keep marriages intact. You can know when your husband has a developing story. It is wise to know what the story is about and discuss the matter before worst comes to worst. Love your in-laws just the way they are. There is no day where your husband will say his people are bad.

Don't bother with anybody who calls you names as long as your husband loves you. Babies keep mothers too busy to listen to nonsense. House girls are the enemies of happily married couples. They give married men extended hospitality—more so than their wives—just to break their marriages. Every woman knows her husband better than anybody else socially. Immoral men are crazy for women. They rape even their own daughters. Love your husband more than anybody else. Your kids will grow and leave you, but your husband will be beside you all your years until death. Immoral men destroy their own marriages. Married women have to pray to God for their marriages to stand. Is your husband having an affair with another woman? Ask him with love when he is in the right mood. If he keeps quiet, withdraw the topic without pushing him. The humbleness of a woman may make her husband reform some days.

It is not wise to be rude to your husband. There is no woman who can imagine sharing her husband with another woman. A married woman must be satisfied with the love given by her husband. Sex is seasonal, but your marriage is for many years. Age or sickness may keep married couples from enjoying sex in their marriage. Personal grooming should be addressed with love in every marriage because it is important. As a married woman, you have to change your attitude toward your husband and neighbors. Be clean and enjoy your marriage because a clean surrounding makes life lovely. If a Miss World decides to be dirty today, no one can recognize her beauty. A foolish woman bewitches her own kids with her tongue. The brain of a child is like a computer; it accepts and downloads any file. Young girls clothe themselves, speak, and behave exactly like their mothers.

Do you allow your daughters to wear miniskirts? Do you go to drinking and cocktail parties with your kids? Why do you allow your mature daughters to play weird games with men where they are half-naked, like prostitutes? Why do you allow your big kids to enter your bedroom without knocking the door? Kids have to know right from wrong as they grow.

Why do you share the same bedroom with your mature kids? Don't capitalize on poverty because privacy is for all classes of people. Do you monitor what is happening between your house girl, husband, and kids in your house? Do you go to church with the community living in your house? Do you pray together with the people living in your house? Do you teach your kids how to pray? Do you speak evil about God and pastors before your kids? Do you pray for God to have mercy upon your husband, or do you help satan kill him? Your marriage will stand by the grace of the Lord in Jesus's name.

Revealed secrets behind relationships and marriages

I saw a man I knew in a dream. He wanted to rape his daughter, Carol, who was born out of wedlock. Carol and her mother could not believe the man they called "Dad" for years would attempt to rape her. He said only sex would satisfy him. Scared, Carol took refuge at her grandmother's house.

I woke up, rebuking the demonic spirits of confusion and incest that were ruling that territory in Jesus's mighty name.

It is the responsibility of every mother to give her grown-up daughters moral support in Jesus's name. Fathers should consider the amount of hugging or kissing they give their daughters when they reach a certain age in life. Mothers must teach their daughters the importance of dressing decently. Whenever immoral men see the private parts of a woman, regardless of age and their relationship to her, they think of sex. A daughter who makes love with her father is cursed because she has seen the nakedness of her father and shared a man with her mother. As a mother, you have to teach your daughters the value of sitting down properly and covering their private parts at all times.

In a dream, I saw a naked woman with long hair swimming from one corner of the sea to another like a fish. She was not a mermaid because I could see her clearly. She was burning with lust from what I could understand in the dream. She didn't look like the girlfriends I'd had before getting saved. I stood at the edge of a very big sea in the spiritual world. I followed the direction of the light, which was like a spotlight coming from the sky. The water mass was still and quiet. I destroyed her immorality and witchcraft in Jesus's name. She went back to the abyss, frustrated that the Holy Spirit of God had destroyed all her evil plans in Jesus's name.

Not all dreams you see are from the Holy Spirit of God. All nightmares come from the dark world. When you romance or have sex with people you know in your dreams, it is demonic spirits you are with. The woman I saw in the deep sea was the queen of the sea. She breaks relationships and marriages by making love with men and women in their dreams. The queen of the sea possesses men with demonic spirits of prostitution and women with demons of lesbianism. Someone who enters your bedroom or bathroom in a dream without fearing your spouse is the spirit of immorality and confusion. Someone who sleeps between married couples in a dream is the spirit of witchcraft and rejection. Making love with dead spirit in your dreams is the spirit of witchcraft and rejection. Being expectant in your dreams is the spirit of witchcraft and barrenness. Whatever the Holy Spirit of God reveals is no longer a weapon to fight your life in Jesus's name. For you to receive deliverance, you have to reveal the secrets you know about the satanic kingdom to your spiritual leader in Jesus's name. There is power in confession because it is a point of surrender to God and people.

In a dream, when you give birth alone in a dirty hut on a bed, this represents the generational curses of poverty and rejection. When you have labor pains without a baby or breastfeeding spiritual babies in your dreams, this represents the generational curses of barrenness and witchcraft. A snake touching a woman's thighs or making love with her spiritually represents the spirit of witchcraft and immorality. Someone marking or painting your face or any other part of your body with different colors in a dream represents the spirit of witchcraft and skin diseases. Someone laughing at you in a dream because you are naked or wearing dirty rags represents the spirit of witchcraft and madness. When you walk with dead spirits in your dreams, regardless of your relationship to them, this represents the spirit of witchcraft and confusion. When you cause accidents in your dreams, this represents the spirit of witchcraft. When a wedding ceremony turns into funeral in a dream, this represents the spirit of witchcraft and sadness.

If you see your legs and hands tied with a rope backward by your spouse or fiancée in a dream, it represents generational curses of rejection. Someone can be married spiritually by spiritual beings without his or her knowledge. Wet dreams are from the dark world. There is no captive who can set himself or herself free from satanic bondage. He or she needs someone stronger from the outside who can speak to his or her spiritual world in Jesus's name. If you have the fear of suffocating or killing your own baby in a dream, this represents the spirit of witchcraft and murder. You have to speak the opposite of the devil's report in your life with your own tongue in Jesus's name.

If people beat you up in your dreams, this represents the generational curses of rejection and hatred. If people laugh at you in your dreams, saying you will never marry, this represents generational curses of rejection. The devil can use anybody, regardless of your relationship to them, to hurt your feelings. Don't listen to what witches say about your life; focus on what the Word of God says about you in Jesus's name.

When fear possesses someone's spirit, he or she becomes confused. This gives the devil a chance to destroy his or her life because there is no more faith in God. Seeing writings like "I love you" in your dreams represents the spirit of confusion from the dark world. Hearing satanic voices say, "You are my husband or wife," in a dream represents the spirit of confusion from the dark world. Any time you see a serpent in your dreams, you have seen satan himself.

Someone cutting your hair or cloth, scaring you with a gun or flames of fire in a dream is the spirit of witchcraft. Satan has no power over your spirit or body—in Jesus's name—because your life was predestined before you were born. If you receive a wedding ring in a dream, this represents the spirit of rejection. If you dance or kiss in the sea in a dream, this represents the generational curses of immorality. A dog wanting to rape someone in a dream represents the spirit of prostitution. If you see people or animals making love in a dream, this represents generational curses of immorality. Someone masturbating—either physically or in the spiritual world—represents the generational curses of immorality and rejection. If you hear romantic noises of guys making love in your dreams, this represents the spirit of rape and prostitution. If you swim in the water in your dreams, this represents the spirit of struggle.

Have you sealed the deal with satan? What is your mission? How is the devil using you? Are you happy to work for the satanic kingdom? The battle is in your heart. No one can make you change your decision; only you can do that. Come to Jesus the way you are. God can use you to bring glory to his kingdom in Jesus's name. Are you tired of working for the satanic kingdom? Come back to the kingdom of God, and you will get peace in Jesus's name.

Stop blaming your spouse or fiancée because of spiritual things he or she could not control. Spouses agree to disagree and look for lasting solutions in every family. The devil is not happy when married couples are happy. Stop blaming each other in a marriage. Blame satan because he is the father of all lies. Don't be afraid. God will fix your relationship and marriage in Jesus's name.

God will give you patience and humility in Jesus's name. Redemption for your marriage only comes when you get saved. Stop living a double-dealing life because God is righteous. Ask God in a prayer to direct you to your Miss or Mr. Right in a divine way. Disconnect yourself from your old lovers permanently in Jesus's name if you want to be happy in your present relationship or marriage. Many married couples live with regret because they didn't want to get out of a relationship early. When you can't take it anymore in your relationship and marriage, you start telling friends and relatives how you can't stand your spouse. Good friends and relatives may try to help you sort out your differences so you can be happy again. The majority of couples may open a dialogue and forgive each other, while others may say it's too late for reconciliation. Divorce and remarriage may not be the end of all troubles in your life socially. Whatever forced you out of your first marriage may follow you into your second marriage. It is only God who can give a man or a woman the grace to love his or her spouse in and out of seasons.

You can exchange anything of this world with relatives and friends, but not your spouse. You can only keep your relationship or marriage by the grace of God because every marriage has wrangles. You don't know why God brought your spouse your way. Do you think you will forget your spouse forever after a divorce? If you share kids or properties, you can't have peace. Marriage judges can't deliver someone from generational curses of immorality. It is only God who can give a married couple the courage to face challenges together for the sake of their kids.

Marrying a younger man or woman can't stop prostitution in someone's life because it is a spirit. Why do you want to separate from your spouse? Do you remember the good things you shared together as a couple? Can you answer the questions your kids will ask your spouse after you have divorced? Are you comfortable being with another man or woman when your former husband or wife struggles with kids? Do you think your former spouse and kids will forgive you in the future after hurting them that much? Before making some big life decisions, you have to think twice because you may need to explain what happened in the future to the parties concerned.

No one likes to encounter misfortune in life. Don't allow your parent or friends to destroy your happiness socially. Parents—especially in Africa—view their working daughters as assets without considering their happiness. There is no time where a father will marry his daughter or a mother will share her husband with her daughter. Let your daughter get married and have kids like her age-mates. A mean parent makes sure his or her daughter separates from any boyfriend she brings home. Single women get frustrated with age more than men do. Your son may take his time to get married, but not your daughter.

Your daughter may take a wrong turn without your knowledge because of frustration in life. It is not a sin biblically for a man or a woman who is of age to start a relationship. An individual can decide to be celibate or marry per the directions of the Holy Spirit of God. Parents should thank God for their sons and daughters who are in healthy relationships and marriages in Jesus's name.

Married couples must love their spouses in all situations. Marriage is not seasonal but for life. Your sons and daughters can abandon you because of sicknesses, but your spouse can't. Never allow your kids to see your ill spouse naked as long as you are alive because it is a curse. I know it is very hard to nurse a spouse with a terminal disease. It is only God who can reward you for being there for your spouse during trying moments in life. Many people didn't marry because they were prepared to marry but because they decided to marry at that time. It is good to marry when you are young and healthy, can start responsibilities early, and have enough strength to hustle for your kids.

People should respect married couples and support them as much as they can in Jesus's name. What do people call happiness in marriage? Learn to take everything to God in prayer, no matter what situation your relationship or marriage might be passing through. You can lose a career and decide to start another one. Biblically, you are not allowed to divorce and marry again as long as your spouse is alive. When a man and a woman join in holy matrimony, God blesses them with kids. This carries their name to the next generation. God will keep your relationship and marriage intact regardless of other situations in Jesus's name. Keep holding on by faith. Don't lose hope.

"Then the Lord God made a woman from the rib he had taken out of the man, and he brought her to the man. The man said, 'This is now bone of my bones and flesh of my flesh; she shall be called "woman," for she was taken out of man.' That is why a man leaves his father and mother and is united to his wife, and they become one flesh" (Genesis 2:22-24, NIV).

www.ingramcontent.com/pod-product-compliance
Lightning Source LLC
Chambersburg PA
CBHW021158080526
44588CB00008B/404